101 THINGS® TO DO WITH A
TORTILLA

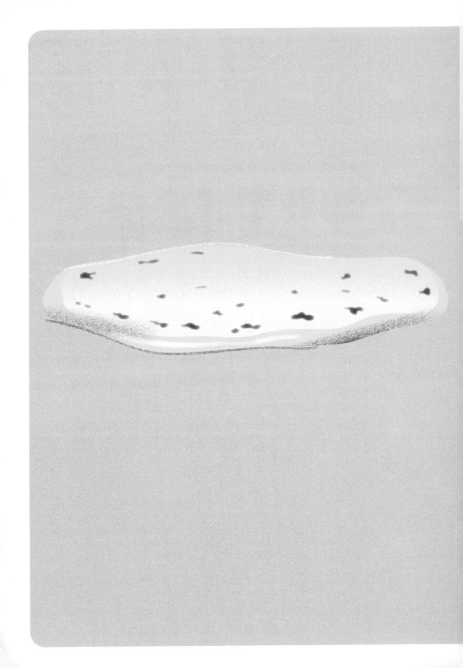

101 THINGS® TO DO WITH A
TORTILLA

STEPHANIE ASHCRAFT
AND DONNA KELLY

Gibbs Smith

Second Edition
27 26 25 24 23   5 4 3 2 1

First Gibbs Smith edition published in 2005
Second Gibbs Smith edition published November 2023

Published by
Gibbs Smith
P.O. Box 667
Layton, Utah 84041

1.800.835.4993 orders
www.gibbs-smith.com

Cover art by Nicole LaRue and Ryan Thomann
Designed by Ryan Thomann and Renee Bond
Printed and bound in China
Gibbs Smith books are printed on either recycled, 100% post-consumer
waste, FSC-certified papers or on paper produced from sustainable PEFC-
certified forest/controlled wood source. Learn more at www.pefc.org.

Library of Congress has cataloged the first edition as follows:
Ashcraft, Stephanie.
101 things to do with a tortilla / Stephanie Ashcraft and Donna Kelly.—1st ed.
p. cm.
ISBN 978-1-58685-469-0 (first edition)
1. Tortillas. I. Title: One hundred and one things to do with a tortilla.
II. Kelly, Donna. III. Title.
TX770.T65A84 2004
641.8'2—dc22
2004020953

ISBN: 978-1-4236-6376-8

With love and admiration to the domestic goddesses who have inspired me: Carol, Carol Ann, Ruby, Glad, Joann, Lisa, June, Karen, Noretta, Sandy, and especially for Anne, Kathleen, and Amelia.—D. K.

Thanks to all my family for their support, and to my college roommates—Felicia, who introduced me to cooking with tortillas, and Royleane, who got me excited about cooking in the first place.—S. A.

CONTENTS

Helpful Hints

- Corn tortillas come in a standard 6-inch size. Generally, they must be cooked before being eaten. Heat an 8-inch or larger skillet on the stove top and lay a tortilla on the hot pan. With a spatula, flip the tortilla every 30–45 seconds, or until lightly toasted but bendable.

- Flour tortillas come ready to eat in a variety of shapes and sizes. In this book, we refer to flour tortillas in three sizes: small (6- to 7-inch diameter, often called "taco size"); medium (8- to 10-inch diameter, and most common size); and large (11- to 14-inch diameter, often called "burrito size").

- Flour tortillas come in a variety of thicknesses, including an extra thick version called "gordita-style." These are heavier than average flour tortillas and are often used in recipes that require baking, such as for main dishes.

- Flour tortillas often come in a variety of flavors, such as wheat, tomato, or spinach. These may be substituted for regular flour tortillas in any recipe, but baking times may need to be adjusted, and the flavor will be a little different.

- To prevent tortillas from cracking or breaking, soften them in the microwave before using. Place up to 4 tortillas at a time on a plate and cover with a paper towel. Microwave 20–30 seconds, or until tortillas are soft and bendable. Keep covered with paper towel until ready to use.

- Tortillas store well in the refrigerator for about 2 weeks or in the freezer 2–3 months. Always store opened tortillas in an airtight container.

- Rolling styles for tortillas vary according to each recipe. Generally, jelly roll style means rolling the tortilla in a tight roll with both ends open. Burrito style means folding the ends in and then rolling the tortilla in a large roll, with no openings.

- The first time you try baking a recipe, check the food 3–5 minutes before its minimum cooking time ends—each oven heats differently, so cooking time can vary.

- For the health conscious, low-fat or light ingredients can be used in all recipes.

APPETIZERS

Football Bean Dip

MAKES 6–8 SERVINGS

1 can (16 ounces)	refried beans
²⁄₃ cup	sour cream
¹⁄₃ cup	Miracle Whip
2 tablespoons	taco seasoning
2 cups	shredded lettuce
2	Roma tomatoes, chopped
2	green onions, sliced
1 can (2.25 ounces)	sliced black olives
1 cup	grated cheddar cheese
1 bag (16 ounces)	tortilla chips

Spread refried beans on bottom of an 8 x 8-inch pan. In a bowl, mix sour cream, Miracle Whip, and taco seasoning together. Spread over beans. Layer lettuce, tomatoes, green onions, olives, and cheese over top. Stand a line of tortilla chips around the sides of the pan as a garnish. Place remaining chips in a serving bowl.

Tortilla Sushi Rolls

MAKES 12 ROLLS

2	medium flour tortillas
4 tablespoons	cream cheese, softened
1 cup	cooked white rice
½ cup	cooked crabmeat
½	avocado, sliced lengthwise into 8 strips
2 tablespoons	finely diced green onion or green pepper
½ cup	sour cream, mixed with 2 teaspoons Tabasco sauce

Cut tortillas to form a 6-inch square and warm in microwave until just softened. Spread cream cheese in a thin layer over tortillas. Spoon rice over half of each tortilla. Place crabmeat, avocado, and green onion lengthwise over rice. Roll up tightly, jelly roll style. Cut into 1-inch pieces. Lay pieces flat on a baking sheet. Drizzle with sour cream and Tabasco sauce mixture. Broil 3–5 minutes. Store leftovers in refrigerator.

Smoked-Salmon Triangles

MAKES 24 TRIANGLES

4 tablespoons	**butter, divided**
4	**medium flour tortillas**
1 package (8 ounces)	**cream cheese, softened**
½ pound	**thinly sliced smoked salmon**
2	**medium tomatoes, thinly sliced**
1	**medium purple onion, thinly sliced**
	fresh parsley, chopped

Melt 1 tablespoon butter in a frying pan over low heat. Cook 1 tortilla until light golden brown and crisp on one side only. Remove and cool. Repeat with remaining tortillas. Divide cream cheese into four equal parts and spread over each tortilla on the noncrisp side. Then equally divide and add salmon, tomatoes, and onion. Cut each tortilla into six triangle wedges. Chill before serving. Garnish with freshly chopped parsley.

Tortilla Pinwheels
MAKES 24 PINWHEELS

2 packages (8 ounces each)	cream cheese, softened
2 tablespoons	mustard
6	large flour tortillas
2 pounds	thinly sliced deli turkey
4 cups	chopped fresh spinach
1	red pepper, finely chopped
2 cups	grated cheese, any type

Combine cream cheese and mustard. Spread ⅓ cup cream cheese mixture over each tortilla. Layer turkey, spinach, pepper, and cheese onto half of each tortilla. Roll up jelly roll style. Wrap individually in plastic wrap and chill at least 1 hour. Slice each roll into 2-inch pieces and arrange on a platter. Serve chilled.

Tortilla Garnishes

Tortilla Matchsticks:

MAKES 2 CUPS

With a pizza cutter, slice 2 medium flour tortillas into very thin matchstick pieces. Spread on a baking sheet and bake 5–6 minutes at 400 degrees. Stir. Return to oven 3–5 minutes more. Matchsticks should be crisp and golden brown. Cool.

Tortilla Crisps:

MAKES 2 CUPS

With a pizza cutter, cut 3 corn or 2 medium flour tortillas into small rectangles. Heat canola oil in a small frying pan over medium heat. Add a small amount of tortilla rectangles to pan. They will cook quickly. Cool on a plate covered with a paper towel. Blot carefully to remove excess oil.

Tortilla Confetti:

MAKES 2 CUPS

Purchase flour tortillas of different colors at the deli section of a grocery store. With kitchen scissors or a pizza cutter, cut 2 medium tortillas into tiny squares. Use as they are, or follow Tortilla Matchsticks directions above for crispy tortilla confetti.

Migas (Tortilla Crumbs):

Using the leftover tortilla crumbs at the bottom of a bag of tortilla chips, crush with a rolling pin or fork. Sprinkle over main dishes, salads, or soups as an easy last-minute garnish.

Never-Fail Nachos

MAKES 3–5 SERVINGS

> **8 cups   tortilla chips**
> **2 cups   grated cheddar cheese**

Preheat oven to 475 degrees. Spread tortilla chips in a
9 x 13-inch pan or on a baking sheet. Sprinkle cheese over
top. Place in oven on center rack 1–3 minutes, or until cheese
is melts. Remove from oven and top with desired toppings
as listed below. Return pan to center of oven and broil
3–5 minutes, or until bubbly and hot.

College Survival variation: Spread 1 can (16 ounces)
refried beans evenly over chips and cheese. Broil as
directed above. Remove from oven and garnish with
salsa, guacamole, and/or sour cream, if desired.

Barbecue Chicken variation: Dice 2 barbecued
chicken breasts. Sprinkle over chips and cheese.
Chop ½ red onion and sprinkle over top. Broil as
directed above. Remove from oven, drizzle spicy
barbecue sauce on top, and garnish with chopped
cilantro and tomatoes.

Taco-Style variation: Cook ½ pound ground beef
seasoned with chili powder and garlic salt, to taste.
Spoon meat on top of chips and cheese. Broil as
directed above. Remove from oven and sprinkle with
shredded lettuce, chopped tomatoes, and salsa.

Pepper Jelly Bites

MAKES 36 BITES

6	medium flour tortillas
6 tablespoons	cream cheese, softened
6 tablespoons	jalapeño pepper jelly
$3/4$ cup	finely chopped pecans

Cut each tortilla into a 6-inch square, then spread with
1 tablespoon cream cheese. Spread 1 tablespoon jelly over
cream cheese, then sprinkle each tortilla with 2 tablespoons
pecans. Roll up jelly roll style. Wrap individually with clear
plastic wrap and refrigerate at least 1 hour. When ready to
serve, remove plastic wrap and slice into 1-inch rolls.

Mini Guacamole Cups

MAKES 12 MINI TORTILLA CUPS

2	large ripe avocados, peeled and seeded
1 tablespoon	lime juice
2 tablespoons	minced white onion
¼ teaspoon	salt
3	large, thin flour tortillas

Preheat the oven to 400 degrees. Cut tortillas into 12 (3-inch) circles. Lightly spray both sides of the circles with oil. Press each circle into a mini muffin cup, with sides rippled and slightly overlapping to form a cup shape. Bake for 8–10 minutes, until golden brown.

Mash avocados right before serving. Stir in lime juice, onion, and salt. Spoon a little guacamole into each tortilla cup.

Southwest Egg Rolls
MAKES 12 EGG ROLLS

12	corn tortillas
	canola oil, for frying
2 cups	shredded cabbage
2 cups	chopped spinach
2 tablespoons	butter
1/2 cup	corn
1/2 cup	cooked black beans
1 cup	grated pepper jack cheese
1 small jar	sweet-and-sour sauce

Cut tortillas into 6-inch squares and warm in microwave 60 seconds on a plate covered with a dishcloth.

Heat about 2 inches of oil in a small saucepan over medium heat.

In a small frying pan, sauté cabbage and spinach in butter until just limp, not browned. Remove from heat and mix in corn, black beans, and cheese. Place 2 tablespoons of mixture on a tortilla and roll into an egg roll shape. Place seam-side down in hot oil in saucepan. Cook until golden brown on both sides. Serve hot with sweet-and-sour sauce for dipping.

Spinach and Cheese Triangles

MAKES 18 TRIANGLES

1 cup	chopped green onion
½ cup	butter, melted
2 tablespoons	minced garlic
1 bag (16 ounces)	frozen chopped spinach, thawed and drained
2 cups	crumbled feta cheese or queso fresco
2	eggs, beaten
6	large, thin flour tortillas

Preheat oven to 350 degrees. Sauté green onion in ¼ cup butter for 1 minute. Add garlic and sauté 2 minutes more. Add spinach and stir frequently until all moisture evaporates. Remove from heat. Stir in cheese and eggs.

Cut tortillas into 3 x 10-inch strips (about three per tortilla). Place 2 tablespoons spinach mixture on one end of a strip, and fold into a triangle, like folding a flag. Place on baking sheet, seam-side down. Brush each tortilla with melted butter. Bake 20 minutes, or until light golden brown.

Tortilla Flats

MAKES 48 APPETIZERS

12	**medium gordita-style flour tortillas**
1 container (8 ounces)	**spreadable garlic-and-herb cheese**
	chopped vegetables and meat

Using 2-inch-round cookie cutters, cut circles out of tortillas.*
Place four circles on a plate and microwave 30 seconds.
Remove tortillas and press flat with a dish towel to remove
any bubbles. Wipe moisture off plate. Replace tortilla rounds
on plate. Microwave another 30 seconds, or until crisp, but
not brown.

Spread a thin layer of cheese on top of each round.
Then place chopped vegetables and meat, as desired.
Recommended meats are smoked chicken chunks or grilled
shrimp. Recommended vegetables are chopped fresh green
and red chiles, grated jicama with lime and seasoned salt,
or sliced cherry tomatoes.

*Festive holiday cookie cutters such
as stars or hearts may be used.

QUESADILLAS & WRAPS

Bean 'n' Cheese Quesadillas

MAKES 3–5 SERVINGS

1 can (16 ounces)	refried beans
10	medium flour tortillas
1^2/$_3$ cups	taco-blend grated cheese
^{3}/$_4$ cup	green taco sauce
^{1}/$_2$ cup	chopped green onion
	fresh salsa and/or guacamole

Heat refried beans and spread evenly over 5 tortillas. On each tortilla, sprinkle ^{1}/$_3$ cup cheese over bean layer, followed by 2 tablespoons taco sauce and some green onion. Place remaining 5 tortillas over top. Cook over medium heat in a frying pan until light golden brown. Flip and toast other side. Cut quesadillas into six wedges with a pizza cutter. Serve with fresh salsa and/or guacamole.

Tomato-Olive Quesadillas

MAKES 4–6 SERVINGS

1 can (2.25 ounces)	chopped olives
1 cup	chopped green onion
1	medium tomato, chopped
1 cup	grated mozzarella cheese
1 cup	grated cheddar cheese
12	small flour tortillas
	guacamole, sour cream, and/or salsa

Evenly divide and layer the olives, onion, tomato, and cheeses on top of 6 tortillas; then place remaining 6 tortillas over top. Lightly toast over medium heat in a frying pan. Turn over every 30 seconds until tortilla is golden brown on both sides. Cut each tortilla into six wedges with a pizza cutter. Serve with guacamole, sour cream, and/or salsa.

Italian Roast Beef Wraps
MAKES 1–2 SERVINGS

2	large flour tortillas
6 to 8	slices roast beef
2	slices Provolone cheese, cut in half
1 cup	shredded lettuce
1	medium tomato, chopped
¼	medium red or yellow onion, thinly sliced
2 to 3 tablespoons	Italian salad dressing

Place tortillas on microwave-safe plates. Divide roast beef and lay over each tortilla. Lay cheese halves from top to bottom in the center of each tortilla. Microwave each tortilla 45–55 seconds, or until cheese melts. Divide lettuce, tomato, and onion evenly over melted cheese. Drizzle dressing over top. Fold in the ends of each tortilla, then roll in the sides to form a burrito-style wrap.

Mandarin Chicken Wraps

MAKES 2–4 SERVINGS

2	boneless, skinless chicken breasts
	Asian seasoning or cumin
	olive or vegetable oil
	salt and pepper, to taste
4	large flour tortillas
1 package (8 ounces)	cream cheese, softened
1 can (8 ounces)	mandarin oranges, drained
⅓ cup	chopped green onion
1 cup	chow mein noodles
8	red lettuce leaves

Season chicken with your favorite Asian seasoning or cumin. Brown chicken breasts in a small amount of oil until chicken is completely cooked. Season with salt and pepper. Remove chicken from pan. Spread cream cheese over each tortilla. Using two forks, shred chicken, and then divide evenly over tortillas, leaving at least 1 inch uncovered on one side. Sprinkle oranges, onion, and chow mein noodles over chicken. Lay lettuce over top. Fold in the ends of each tortilla, then roll in the sides to form a burrito-style wrap. Serve immediately or wrap individually in plastic wrap and refrigerate for later use.

Turkey-Swiss Spinach Wraps

MAKES 3–5 SERVINGS

1	large avocado, peeled and seeded*
1 pinch	salt
5	large spinach tortillas
10	slices turkey breast lunch meat
5	slices Swiss cheese
2	medium tomatoes, diced
3 cups	shredded lettuce

Mash avocado with a fork. Stir salt into avocado, and then spread evenly over tortillas. Lay 2 turkey slices over each tortilla, covering tortilla as much as possible. Cut each slice of cheese in half; then lay over meat. Sprinkle tomato and lettuce in center of each tortilla. Roll tortilla jelly roll style and secure with a toothpick. Serve immediately or wrap individually in plastic wrap and refrigerate for later use.

*2 small avocados may be substituted.

#17

Teriyaki Fish Wraps

MAKES 6–8 SERVINGS

3 cans (8 ounces each)	tuna or other whitefish fillets
1 jar (12 ounces)	teriyaki marinade
2 tablespoons	canola oil
¾ cup	sour cream
¾ cup	honey mustard salad dressing
8	large flour tortillas
2 cups	chopped lettuce
1	medium red onion, finely diced
2	medium tomatoes, diced

Cut fish fillets into chunks and marinate in teriyaki sauce at least 2 hours. In a frying pan, sauté fish in oil until heated through. Combine sour cream and dressing. Warm tortillas in microwave. Spread dressing mixture on tortillas. Add fish, lettuce, onion, and tomato. Fold in the ends of each tortilla then roll in the sides to form a burrito-style wrap.

Variation: Use chicken instead of fish.

Tuna Melt Triangles

MAKES 2–3 SERVINGS

3	medium gordita-style flour tortillas
1 can (12 ounces)	tuna, drained
1 package (8 ounces)	cream cheese, softened
1 cup	finely grated mozzarella cheese
½ cup	Parmesan cheese
1 tablespoon	dried parsley
1 teaspoon	lemon juice

Preheat oven to 350 degrees. Cut each tortilla into quarters. Place triangles directly onto oven rack and bake 6–8 minutes. Turn triangles over and bake another 3–5 minutes, or until crisp and golden brown. Remove from oven.

Mix remaining ingredients together; spread evenly on each tortilla triangle. Place on a baking sheet and put on center oven rack. Broil 2–3 minutes, or until mixture is bubbly and golden brown.

Open-Face Pesto Quesadillas

MAKES 2–4 SERVINGS

2 cups	**grated cheddar cheese**
4	**medium flour tortillas**
1 small jar (6 ounces)	**pesto sauce**
2	**small tomatoes, thinly sliced**
1	**cooked chicken breast, thinly sliced (optional)**
½ cup	**pine nuts or slivered almonds**

Preheat oven to 350 degrees. Sprinkle cheese over 2 tortillas and place remaining tortillas on top. Place in oven directly on rack and bake 6–8 minutes. Remove from oven and press tortilla flat with a clean dish towel to remove any air bubbles. Turn over and bake 3–5 minutes more. Remove from oven. Layer pesto sauce, tomatoes, chicken, if desired, and nuts over each tortilla. Broil in oven until hot and bubbly.

BLT Wraps

MAKES 1–2 SERVINGS

2	medium wheat tortillas
2 tablespoons	mayonnaise or Miracle Whip
4 to 6	slices bacon, cooked
1 cup	shredded lettuce
1	medium tomato, diced

Place tortillas on plates. Spread mayonnaise over each tortilla. Divide bacon and layer over center of each tortilla. Sprinkle lettuce and tomato over top. Fold in the ends of each tortilla, then roll in the sides to form a burrito-style wrap.

#21

Chicken Caesar Wraps

MAKES 4–6 SERVINGS

2	chicken breasts, cooked and chilled
6 cups	chopped romaine lettuce
1/2 cup	Caesar salad dressing
1 cup	grated Parmesan cheese
6	large flour tortillas

Cut chicken breasts into small cubes. Toss lettuce in dressing. Place lettuce, cheese, and chicken evenly over tortillas. Fold in the ends of each tortilla, then roll in the sides to form a burrito-style wrap.

Chicken Quesadilla Stacks

MAKES 6–8 SERVINGS

1	red pepper, chopped
1 pint (16 ounces)	sour cream
3 cups	shredded cooked chicken
2 cups	grated zucchini
2 cups	grated green pepper
6 tablespoons	butter, divided
8	medium flour tortillas
2 cups	grated Monterey Jack cheese
	sour cream
	salsa

Preheat oven to 350 degrees. Puree red pepper in a blender; then combine with sour cream in a bowl and set aside.

Sauté chicken, zucchini, and green pepper in 2 tablespoons butter. Cook 5 minutes, or until vegetables are tender. Remove from heat and drain excess liquid. Add sour cream sauce.

Place 2 tortillas on a baking sheet. Spread 1/2 tablespoon butter on each tortilla and ladle 2/3 cup chicken mixture over top, spreading to the edges. Sprinkle with 1/4 cup cheese. Repeat this process three more times, ending with cheese on top. Bake 15 to 20 minutes, or until heated through and bubbly. Cut each tortilla stack into four wedges. Serve with a dollop of sour cream and salsa.

KIDS
&
SNACKS

Happy Clown Faces

MAKES 6 FACES

3 tablespoons	butter
6	corn tortillas
6 tablespoons	cinnamon sugar
1 container (8 ounces)	whipped cream cheese, softened
	sliced fruits
	coconut
	nuts
	chocolate chips

In a small frying pan, sauté each tortilla in $\frac{1}{2}$ tablespoon butter until light golden brown and crisp. Remove, sprinkle with cinnamon sugar, and cool. Spread lightly with cream cheese. Let each child make a face by placing fruit, coconut, nuts, and chocolate chips over cream cheese.

Tortilla Snowflakes

MAKES 6 SNOWFLAKES

6	**large thin flour tortillas**
1 cup	**chocolate nut spread (like Nutella)**
1 cup	**powdered sugar**

Place each tortilla in the microwave 20–30 seconds, or until softened. Remove from microwave and fold in half, then fold in half again. Cut a design into folded tortilla, just like cutting a paper snowflake. Open up, place tortilla snowflake on a plate, and microwave 30 seconds. Take tortilla off the plate, wipe off any excess moisture, and let cool. Tortilla should be crisp but not brown, so if necessary, microwave for an additional 20 seconds at a time until crisp.. Place tortilla on a sheet of wax paper. Using a small paintbrush, paint chocolate spread on tortilla. Dust each snowflake generously with powdered sugar.

#25
Tortilla Elephant Ears

MAKES 6–8 SERVINGS

2 cups	**canola oil, for frying**
8	**medium gordita-style flour tortillas**
2 tablespoons	**cinnamon**
1 cup	**sugar**

Heat oil over medium heat in a frying pan. Fry each tortilla in oil, turning over until light golden brown on each side. Do not crisp. Mix together cinnamon and sugar. Spread sugar mixture on a large plate. Using tongs, remove tortilla from pan and immediately press each side of tortilla into sugar mixture. Serve warm.

Variation: Use festive holiday cookie cutters to cut holes in tortilla before frying. For Halloween, cut a jack-o'-lantern face in tortilla before frying.

Creamy Fruit Roll-Ups
MAKES 1 SERVING

2 tablespoons	**cream cheese**
1	**medium flour tortilla**
¹⁄₂ cup	**finely chopped fruit**

Spread cream cheese on tortilla and sprinkle with fruit. Strawberries, bananas, crushed pineapple, berries, chopped apples, and mandarin oranges may be used. Roll up tortilla, jelly roll style.

Variation: Use fruity jams instead of chopped fruit.

Ham-and-Cheese Roll

MAKES 1 SERVING

1	small flour tortilla
1 tablespoon	mayonnaise, mixed with 1 teaspoon mustard
1	slice ham
1	piece string cheese
1	dill pickle, cut lengthwise into quarters

Spread tortilla with mayonnaise and mustard mixture. Top with ham, string cheese, and dill pickle. Roll tortilla up with cheese and pickle in the center.

Variation: Substitute turkey or roast beef for the ham.

Peanut Butter S'mores

MAKES 1 SERVING

1 tablespoon	peanut butter
1	medium flour tortilla
⅛ cup	milk chocolate chips
¼ cup	mini marshmallows

Spread peanut butter over tortilla. Sprinkle chocolate chips and marshmallows over top. Microwave 45 seconds. Allow to cool 3–5 minutes. Roll jelly roll style when cool.

Variation: Substitute grated carrots, apples, raisins, bananas, or crushed pineapple for chocolate chips and marshmallows.

Banana Split Roll

MAKES 1 SERVING

1	medium flour tortilla
2 tablespoons	chocolate nut spread (like Nutella)
2 tablespoons	chopped nuts
2 tablespoons	chopped maraschino cherries
1	medium banana, peeled

Spread tortilla with chocolate spread. Sprinkle nuts and cherries over top. Place banana on one edge of tortilla. Make cuts on the inside curve of the banana so that it can be straightened out. Roll tortilla up, jelly roll style.

Pigs in a Blanket

MAKES 6–8 SERVINGS

1 package (8 count)	hot dogs
4	slices cheddar cheese
4	small gordita-style flour tortillas

Preheat oven to 425 degrees. Make a slice in each hot dog lengthwise. Insert a half slice of cheese in the center of each hot dog. Cut tortillas in half. Wrap one half around each hot dog and secure with a toothpick. Place each tortilla-wrapped hot dog on a baking sheet. Bake 10–12 minutes, or until golden brown.

SOUPS
&
SALADS

#31

Instant Chicken Taco Soup

MAKES 4–6 SERVINGS

1 can (15 ounces)	whole kernel corn, with liquid
1 can (12.5 ounces)	chunk chicken, with liquid
1 can (15 ounces)	black beans, rinsed and drained
1 can (10 ounces)	diced tomatoes with green chiles, with liquid
1 can (14.5 ounces)	chicken broth
1 envelope	taco seasoning mix
1 bag (12 to 16 ounces)	tortilla chips
	grated cheddar cheese

Combine all ingredients except tortilla chips and cheese in a medium saucepan. Bring to a light boil, and remove from heat. Crush desired amount of tortilla chips in bottom of soup bowls. Pour soup over chips. Garnish with cheese.

Chicken Enchilada Soup

MAKES 4–6 SERVINGS

2 cups	chopped cooked chicken breasts
1 tablespoon	butter
$\frac{1}{2}$ cup	diced green onion
1 tablespoon	minced garlic
3 cups	chicken broth
1 can (14 ounces)	enchilada sauce
4	corn tortillas
1 cup	sour cream
2 cups	grated cheddar cheese
	crushed tortilla chips

Sauté chicken in butter. Add onion and garlic and cook until tender. Add broth and enchilada sauce. Cut tortillas into small pieces with a pizza cutter. Add to soup. Simmer 5–10 minutes. Add sour cream and cheese and stir until melted. Serve hot with crushed tortilla chips as a garnish.

Creamy Turkey Tortilla Soup

MAKES 4 SERVINGS

10	corn tortillas
1 can (14 ounces)	chicken broth
1 can (15 ounces)	green enchilada sauce
1 can (10 ounces)	red enchilada sauce
1 teaspoon	cumin
2¼ cups	shredded cooked turkey
1 cup	half-and-half*
	grated cheddar cheese

Cut tortillas into ½ x 3-inch strips. In a saucepan, cook tortilla strips and chicken broth over medium heat until broth thickens and tortillas are soft. Add enchilada sauces and cumin. Mix in turkey and half-and-half. Cook until hot, but do not allow to boil. Garnish individual servings with cheese.

*Whole milk may be substituted.

Do-It-Yourself Tortilla Soup

MAKES 4–6 SERVINGS

12 cups	hot chicken broth
3 cups	cubed cooked chicken
3 cups	grated cheddar cheese
1 cup	Tortilla Matchsticks (see Tortilla Garnishes page 16)
4 cups	finely chopped raw vegetables, such as avocado, onion, green peppers, tomatoes, and olives
	salsa (optional)
	sour cream (optional)

Keep chicken broth simmering in a pan on the stove or in a slow cooker on high heat. Place each remaining ingredient in separate serving bowls. Have each person take an empty bowl and fill with ingredients of their choice. Ladle hot broth over top of ingredients and stir. Top with a handful of Tortilla Matchsticks. Serve with a dollop of salsa or sour cream, if desired.

Green Chile Tortilla Soup

MAKES 4 SERVINGS

1 can (26 ounces)	**chicken and rice soup, condensed**
2 cups	**water**
1 can (10 ounces)	**diced tomatoes with green chiles, with liquid**
	tortilla chips
1 cup	**grated cheddar cheese**

Combine soup, water, and tomatoes in a medium saucepan. Bring to a boil and remove from heat. Crush tortilla chips in bottom of individual soup bowls. Pour soup over chips and sprinkle cheese over top.

Zesty Ranch Bean Tortilla Soup

MAKES 8–10 SERVINGS

5 ½ cups	water
4	boneless, skinless chicken breasts
1	medium onion, chopped
1 can (16 ounces)	kidney beans, drained
1 can (15 ounces)	garbanzo beans, drained
1 can (16 ounces)	pinto beans, drained
1 can (15 ounces)	black beans, rinsed and drained
2 cans (10 ounces each)	diced tomatoes with green chiles, with liquid
1 envelope	taco seasoning
1 envelope	ranch dressing mix
	tortilla chips
	grated Monterey Jack cheese

In a 4-quart soup pan, combine water and chicken, and simmer over medium-high heat 30–45 minutes, or until chicken is cooked through. Remove chicken and cut into bite-size pieces. Return chicken to the broth in pan and stir in onion, beans, tomatoes, taco seasoning, and ranch dressing mix. Simmer 20 minutes over medium-low heat, or until heated through. Serve soup over crushed tortilla chips. Garnish each individual bowl with cheese and a dollop of sour cream.

Festive Confetti Salad

MAKES 4–6 SERVINGS

1 container (16 ounces)	cottage cheese
¼ cup	chopped carrot
¼ cup	chopped onion
¼ cup	chopped red pepper
¼ cup	chopped green pepper
1 can (8 ounces)	pineapple tidbits, drained
1 tablespoon	sugar or sweetener, or to taste
6 cups	blue corn tortilla chips
½ cup	toasted sunflower seeds

Mix cottage cheese, vegetables, pineapple, and sugar. Spread a handful of tortilla chips on a small plate. Top with 1 cup mounded cottage cheese mixture. Sprinkle generously with sunflower seeds. Eat with your fingers, using tortillas as scoops.

Black Bean Guacamole Salad

MAKES 4 SERVINGS

12	whole tortilla chips
4 cups	broken tortilla chips
3 cups	chopped lettuce
1 can (15 ounces)	black beans, rinsed and drained
2 cups	guacamole
1 cup	sour cream, thinned with 1 tablespoon lime juice
	chili powder or paprika

Arrange whole tortilla chips on outside edge of a large plate, pointing out. Spread broken chips on rest of plate. Layer lettuce, black beans, and guacamole over top. Drizzle on sour cream mixture. Sprinkle with chili powder.

Seafood Tostada Salad

MAKES 6 SERVINGS

1 cup	tiny shrimp, cooked and chilled
1½ cups	crabmeat, cooked and chilled
1	ripe avocado, sliced
1 cup	chopped green onion
1 package (8 ounces)	frozen peas
½ cup	vinegar
6 tablespoons	canola oil
1 tablespoon	sugar or sweetener
6	corn tortilla tostada shells
1 can (16 ounces)	refried beans, heated
2 cups	grated cheddar cheese
8 cups	finely chopped lettuce

Mix together shrimp, crabmeat, avocado, green onion, peas, vinegar, oil, and sugar and set aside.

Spread each tostada shell with ¼ cup refried beans and top with ⅓ cup cheese. Place each tostada on a plate. Stir lettuce into seafood mixture, divide into six servings, and mound lettuce mixture onto each tostada. Sprinkle cheese over top.

Taco Salad in a Tortilla Bowl

MAKES 6 SERVINGS

6	large flour tortillas
1 pound	ground beef or turkey
1 tablespoon	chili powder
1 teaspoon	garlic salt
1 can (30 ounces)	refried beans, heated
6 to 8 cups	shredded lettuce
3 cups	chopped tomatoes
3 cups	grated cheddar cheese
	salsa

Preheat oven to 375 degrees. Spray an empty 4- to 5-inch-diameter can or baking pan with nonstick cooking spray. Drape a tortilla over top. Bake 8–10 minutes, or until light golden brown. Let cool 5 minutes before removing tortilla from can or pan. While tortilla is baking, brown meat in spices.

Place tortilla bowls on plates. Spread beans evenly in bottom of each tortilla bowl. Spoon meat on top of beans; layer remaining ingredients over top of meat.

Layered Rainbow Salad

MAKES 6–8 SERVINGS

2 cups	crushed blue corn tortilla chips
1 package (8 ounces)	frozen peas
6	hard-boiled eggs, sliced
2 cups	thinly sliced carrots
2 cups	chopped red peppers
1 cup	chopped purple onion
1 cup	chopped celery
1 cup	mayonnaise
½ cup	sour cream
1 tablespoon	sugar or sweetener

In an 8-inch glass trifle bowl, layer chips, peas, eggs, carrots, and red peppers. Then spread purple onion close to outside of bowl and fill center with celery. Combine mayonnaise, sour cream, and sugar, and spread over top to seal. Cover and refrigerate 1–2 hours. Serve chilled.

Picnic Taco Salad

MAKES 6–8 SERVINGS

1 pound	ground beef
1 envelope	taco seasoning
8 cups	shredded lettuce
2 cups	chopped tomatoes
2 cups	grated cheddar cheese
1 can (15 ounces)	black or pinto beans, rinsed and drained
1 small bottle (14 ounces)	Russian salad dressing
4 cups	crushed corn tortilla chips

Brown meat and add taco seasoning according to directions. Cool. Combine all ingredients except Russian dressing and tortilla chips. Refrigerate 1–2 hours. Add dressing and chips right before serving.

BREAKFAST

Overnight Brunch Enchiladas
MAKES 8–10 SERVINGS

1 bag (16 ounces)	fully cooked cubed ham
$\frac{1}{2}$ cup	sliced green onion
$\frac{3}{4}$ cup	chopped green pepper
10	medium flour tortillas
$2\frac{1}{2}$ cups	grated cheddar cheese, divided
5	large eggs, beaten
2 cups	half-and-half
$\frac{1}{2}$ cup	milk
1 tablespoon	flour
$\frac{1}{2}$ teaspoon	garlic powder
$\frac{1}{2}$ teaspoon	black pepper

Stir together ham, green onion, and green pepper. Spread
$\frac{1}{3}$ cup mixture down middle of each tortilla. Sprinkle
2 tablespoons cheese over top. Roll tortillas and place them,
seam-side down, in bottom of a greased 9 x 13-inch pan.
Mix eggs, half-and-half, milk, flour, garlic powder, and pepper
together. Pour egg mixture evenly over rolled tortillas. Cover
and refrigerate overnight. Preheat oven to 350 degrees. Bake,
uncovered, 50 minutes, or until egg mixture is cooked through.
Sprinkle remaining cheese over enchiladas. Bake an additional
3–5 minutes, or until cheese melts.

Ham-and-Cheese Breakfast Burritos

MAKES 2–4 SERVINGS

3/4 cup	cubed cooked ham
5	large eggs, beaten
1 tablespoon	milk
	salt and pepper, to taste
1/4 cup	grated cheddar cheese
4	medium flour tortillas
	salsa

In a nonstick frying pan sprayed with vegetable oil, cook ham 3–4 minutes. Stir in eggs and milk. Season with salt and pepper. Scramble eggs over medium-low heat until done. Sprinkle cheese over eggs. Roll scrambled eggs in a tortilla. Serve with salsa.

Breakfast Tostada
MAKES 4 SERVINGS

	butter or margarine
4	corn tortillas
1 cup	grated cheddar cheese
2 cups	shredded lettuce
1¼ cups	cubed cooked ham
4	eggs, scrambled
	chopped tomato, sliced olives, and sour cream

Preheat oven to 400 degrees. Spread butter or margarine on one side of each tortilla and lay tortillas butter-side up on a large baking sheet. Bake 3–5 minutes, or until tortillas are toasted. Flip tortillas, then sprinkle cheese over top. Bake 1–2 minutes, or until cheese melts. Layer lettuce, ham, and scrambled eggs over top. Garnish with chopped tomato, sliced olives, and sour cream.

Green Chile Eggs Benedict

MAKES 4 SERVINGS

8	corn tortillas
4 tablespoons	butter
2 cups	hollandaise sauce, divided
4	slices cooked ham or Canadian bacon
8	strips mild green chiles
8	eggs, scrambled, poached, or fried

Sauté each tortilla in $\frac{1}{2}$ tablespoon butter until lightly crisp and golden brown. Place 2 corn tortillas on a plate. Spread a few tablespoons of sauce on top. Top with a slice of meat, 2 chile strips, and 2 cooked eggs. Repeat with remaining tortillas and ingredients. Ladle $\frac{1}{4}$ cup sauce over top. Heat each plate in microwave 90 seconds.

Overnight Breakfast Casserole

MAKES 6–8 SERVINGS

12	eggs
3 cups	milk
1 teaspoon	salt
1 teaspoon	dry mustard
6	medium flour tortillas, torn into small pieces
2 cups	crumbled cooked sausage
1 cup	chopped onion
1 cup	chopped green peppers
2 cups	grated cheddar or Swiss cheese

Mix eggs, milk, salt, and dry mustard together. Pour 1 cup of egg mixture into a greased 9 x 13-inch pan. Layer half of tortilla pieces, sausage, onion, green pepper, and cheese over top. Cover with remaining egg mixture. Layer remaining ingredients over top, ending with cheese. Cover and refrigerate overnight.

When you are ready to bake the casserole, preheat the oven to 350 degrees. Remove the casserole from the refrigerator and let it sit on the counter while the oven is heating. Bake, uncovered, for 40–50 minutes.

#48
Huevos Rancheros Stacks
MAKES 4 SERVINGS

12	corn tortillas
6 cups	enchilada sauce
2 cups	grated cheddar cheese
4 ounces	queso fresco, crumbled
8	eggs, scrambled, poached, or fried
2 cups	chopped onion or green pepper

Dip 3 corn tortillas in enchilada sauce to coat, and stack on a serving plate. Repeat three more times for a total of four serving plates. Sprinkle the tops with some of both cheeses. Place 2 cooked eggs on each stack. Drizzle on more sauce and sprinkle onion or green pepper over top each stack. Top with more cheese. Microwave each plate 60 seconds, or until hot and bubbling.

Coated Tortilla French Toast
MAKES 3–4 SERVINGS

6	eggs
2 cups	milk
1 teaspoon	cinnamon
2 teaspoons	vanilla
6	medium gordita-style flour tortillas
	butter, for cooking

Mix together eggs, milk, cinnamon, and vanilla. Dip each tortilla in egg mixture and place in a frying pan with a little butter over medium heat. Cook about 30 seconds and turn over. Spread 2 tablespoons egg mixture on tortillas. Turn over again. Keep repeating this process until a layer of egg mixture coats each side of tortilla thoroughly and is golden brown and crispy. Serve as you would traditional French toast.

Confetti Breakfast Bake

MAKES 6–8 SERVINGS

12	corn tortillas
1 can (15 ounces)	black beans, rinsed and drained
1 can (15 ounces)	corn, drained
½ cup	chopped green onion
½ cup	chopped red pepper
3 tablespoons	chopped fresh cilantro
1 cup	grated cheddar cheese, divided
2 cups	milk or half-and-half
6	eggs, slightly beaten

Preheat oven to 325 degrees. Arrange 6 tortillas in a lightly greased 9 x 13-inch pan. Tortillas will overlap. Cut remaining tortillas into 1-inch square pieces. Mix pieces with beans, corn, green onion, red pepper, cilantro, and half of cheese. Spoon into pan. Combine milk and eggs. Pour egg mixture over top. Sprinkle with remaining cheese. Cover and refrigerate 4 hours or overnight. Bake 60 minutes, or until eggs are set. Let stand 5 minutes before serving.

Tortilla Quiches

MAKES 4–6 INDIVIDUAL QUICHES

6	small flour tortillas
4	eggs
1 can (12 ounces)	evaporated milk
1 tablespoon	flour
1 teaspoon	salt
½ cup	chopped cooked ham, bacon, or sausage
¼ cup	chopped green onion
1 cup	finely grated Swiss cheese
	salsa
	sour cream

Preheat oven to 350 degrees. Place a tortilla in microwave 20 seconds, or until softened. Spray one side of each tortilla with nonstick cooking spray and press into six (10-ounce) custard baking cups. Tortilla will stick up about ½ inch over the top.

In a small bowl, combine eggs, milk, flour, and salt together and set aside. Divide remaining ingredients, except for the salsa and sour cream, into tortilla cups, ending with cheese on top. Pour egg mixture over top, about ½ cup in each, or until about two-thirds full. Bake 50 minutes, or until set and lightly browned. Remove from oven and cool slightly before serving. Serve with salsa and sour cream as a garnish.

Huevos Migas

MAKES 4–6 SERVINGS

½ cup	chopped green onion
2 tablespoons	butter
8	eggs
1 cup	milk
½ cup	chopped tomato
1 can (4 ounces)	diced green chiles, drained
1 cup	crushed tortilla chips

Sauté onion in butter in a medium frying pan. Mix eggs and milk, and pour into pan. Scramble over medium heat until eggs are set. Add tomato and green chiles, and cook 3 minutes more. Stir in tortilla chips.

#53

Chili Cheese Breakfast Burrito

MAKES 2–4 SERVINGS

4	medium flour tortillas
6	eggs, scrambled
1 can (15 ounces)	chili, heated
1 cup	grated pepper jack cheese
1 cup	salsa

Heat tortillas in microwave 30 seconds, or until softened. Spread eggs, chili, cheese, and salsa evenly over each tortilla. Roll up and serve.

MAIN DISHES

Family Favorite Taco Casserole

MAKES 4–6 SERVINGS

1 pound	ground beef
1	medium onion, finely chopped
2 cans (8 ounces each)	tomato sauce
1 envelope	taco seasoning
10	medium flour tortillas
1 can (10.5 ounces)	cream of chicken soup, condensed
3/4 cup	milk
2 cups	grated cheddar or Mexican-blend cheese

Preheat oven to 350 degrees. In a large frying pan, brown beef and onion together until meat is done and onion is translucent. Drain any excess liquid. Stir tomato sauce and taco seasoning into meat mixture.

Line bottom and sides of a greased 9 x 13-inch pan with 6 flour tortillas. Spread beef mixture over tortilla crust. Place remaining tortillas over top, cutting to fit if necessary, and covering completely. Mix together soup and milk, and pour over top. Sprinkle cheese over casserole. Cover with aluminum foil and bake 15 minutes. Uncover and bake an additional 5 minutes, or until cheese is completely melted.

Casserole can be assembled the night before and stored in the refrigerator until 10 minutes before baking.

Fajita Burgers

MAKES 6 SERVINGS

6 tablespoons	canola oil
1 tablespoon	chili powder
1 teaspoon	white pepper (optional)
6	medium flour tortillas
6 (¼-pound)	ground beef patties
2 cups	sliced red, green, and/or yellow peppers
6	leaves lettuce
1	large tomato, sliced
6	slices cheddar or pepper jack cheese

Heat a large frying pan or outdoor grill. Mix oil and spices in a small dish. Brush one side of each tortilla with oil mixture. Sauté or grill each tortilla until slightly crisp but not hard, about 30 seconds each side. Cook or grill patties, cut them in half, and set aside. Sauté or grill sliced peppers until just cooked, not limp. To assemble burger, place two halves of burger lengthwise down the center of a tortilla. Add some peppers, lettuce, tomato, and cheese over top. Fold tortilla in half to form a giant taco-looking burger.

Variation: Substitute a chicken breast or veggie burger patty for the ground beef.

#56
Southwest Haystacks
MAKES 6–8 SERVINGS

4 cups	**Tortilla Matchsticks (see Tortilla Garnishes page 16)**
8 cups	**cooked white or Spanish rice**
3 cups	**enchilada sauce**
1 can (16 ounces)	**pinto or black beans, drained and rinsed**
4 cups	**chopped cooked chicken or beef**
2 to 3 cups	**grated cheddar cheese**
6 cups	**finely chopped lettuce**
6 cups	**assorted finely chopped vegetables, such as green onion, avocado, tomato, black olives, and peppers**

Place all the ingredients in separate bowls and serve buffet-style. Each person assembles their own "haystack" by starting with a layer of matchsticks, and then rice and sauce. Top with remaining ingredients of choice.

Mushroom Swiss Tortilla Bake

MAKES 6–8 SERVINGS

1 pound	mushrooms, sliced
1 cup	chopped green onion
½ cup	butter
1 can (19 ounces)	enchilada sauce
1 can (15 ounces)	black beans, with liquid
12	corn tortillas
1 pound	Swiss cheese, grated
	sour cream
	salsa

Preheat oven to 350 degrees. Sauté mushrooms and onion in butter until limp. Blend enchilada sauce and black beans in blender until smooth. Pour a little sauce in a 9 x 13-inch pan. Place 6 tortillas in bottom of pan. Spread half of mushroom and onion mixture in pan over tortillas. Pour half of sauce in pan, and sprinkle half of cheese over top. Repeat layers with remaining ingredients, except for sour cream and salsa. Bake 40 minutes, or until bubbly. Serve with a dollop of sour cream and salsa.

Southwest Pizzas

MAKES 4 PIZZAS

8	medium gordita-style flour tortillas
1 jar (18 ounces)	pizza sauce
2 cups	grated mozzarella cheese
	pizza toppings (of choice)
1 cup	Parmesan cheese

Preheat oven to 450 degrees. Spread 3 tablespoons pizza sauce on one side of a tortilla. Press another tortilla on top. Place directly on oven rack in oven. Bake 8 minutes. Remove from oven and press flat with a dish towel to remove air bubbles. Turn over and bake another 2–3 minutes, or until tortillas are crisp and brown. Remove from oven and press flat again. Place on baking sheet and top with pizza sauce, mozzarella cheese, and toppings, as desired. Place in oven on center rack. Broil until toppings are bubbly and hot. Remove from oven and sprinkle with Parmesan cheese.

Southwest Lasagna

MAKES 8–10 SERVINGS

1 container (15 ounces)	ricotta or cottage cheese
1 package (10 ounces)	frozen chopped spinach, thawed and pressed dry
9	medium flour tortillas, torn into small pieces
1 can (19 ounces)	enchilada sauce, mixed with 1 cup salsa
1 cup	sliced black olives
1 pound	cooked hamburger, seasoned with chili powder and salt
½ pound	grated mozzarella cheese
1 cup	Parmesan cheese

Preheat oven to 350 degrees. Spray a 9 x 13-inch pan with nonstick cooking spray. Mix ricotta cheese with spinach. Layer one-third of each ingredient, starting with tortillas, and then ricotta mixture, enchilada sauce mixture, olives, hamburger, and mozzarella cheese. Repeat layers twice more. Sprinkle Parmesan over top. Bake 40–50 minutes, or until heated through.

Black Bean Casserole

MAKES 6 SERVINGS

2 cans (7 ounces each)	**diced green chiles**
2 cups	**frozen corn**
1 cup	**sour cream**
10	**medium flour tortillas, torn into pieces**
2 cans (15 ounces each)	**black beans, with liquid**
2 cups	**grated pepper jack cheese**
2 cups	**salsa**

Preheat oven to 350 degrees. Combine chiles, corn, and sour cream. In a 1$\frac{1}{2}$- to 2-quart casserole dish, layer half of tortilla pieces, beans, sour cream mixture, cheese, and salsa. Repeat with remaining ingredients. Bake 30 minutes, or until bubbly.

Chili Chicken Casserole

MAKES 4–6 SERVINGS

4	boneless, skinless chicken breasts
12	corn tortillas
2 cans (10.5 ounces each)	cream of chicken soup, condensed
½ cup	milk
1	medium onion, chopped
1 can (4 ounces)	chopped green chiles, with liquid
1 can (15 ounces)	chili with beans
2 cups	grated Monterey Jack or cheddar cheese

Preheat oven to 350 degrees. Place chicken in a greased 9 x 13-inch pan. With a pizza cutter, cut tortillas into 1-inch strips. Lay tortilla strips over chicken.

In a large bowl, combine soup, milk, onion, green chiles, and chili. Spread mixture over tortilla layer. Sprinkle cheese evenly over top. Cover with aluminum foil and bake 25 minutes. Uncover and bake an additional 20–25 minutes, or until chicken is completely cooked through.

Chicken Roll-Ups
MAKES 4–6 SERVINGS

4 cups	**cubed cooked chicken**
1 package (8 ounces)	**cream cheese**
1 can (4 ounces)	**diced green chiles, with liquid**
1 teaspoon	**seasoned salt**
8	**medium gordita-style flour tortillas**
¼ cup	**butter, melted**
1 can (10.5 ounces)	**cream of chicken soup, condensed**
½ cup	**milk**

Preheat oven to 350 degrees. Mix chicken, cream cheese, chiles, and salt. Soften a tortilla in microwave 20 seconds. Place ½ cup chicken mixture on tortilla. Fold in the ends of tortilla then roll the sides to form a bundle. Place seam-side down in a greased 9 x 13-inch pan. Repeat for each tortilla. Brush each bundle with melted butter. Bake 30 minutes, or until golden brown. Mix soup and milk in a saucepan over medium heat. Ladle over each bundle before serving.

Lattice-Top Chicken Potpie

MAKES 6–8 SERVINGS

1	**large potato, peeled**
1	**large carrot, peeled and sliced**
1 bag (8 ounces)	**frozen peas**
2 cups	**cubed cooked chicken**
2 cans (10.5 ounces each)	**cream of chicken soup, condensed**
1 cup	**milk**
4	**large flour tortillas**

Preheat oven to 350 degrees. Cut potato into bite-size pieces. Cook in microwave 5 minutes, or until just tender but not thoroughly cooked. Add remaining ingredients except tortillas and stir. Pour into a 2-quart casserole dish.

Wet tortillas with water. Place 2 tortillas together and press firmly. Place on wax paper. Cut into 1-inch-wide strips with a pizza cutter. Lay on top of casserole, weaving together, lattice-style. Repeat with remaining 2 tortillas. Entire dish should be covered with strips. Bake 30 minutes, or until light golden brown.

Polynesian Bundles
MAKES 6–8 SERVINGS

3 cups	frozen hash browns
¼ cup	butter
¾ cup	frozen peas
1	medium onion, finely chopped
1 can (8 ounces)	crushed pineapple, with liquid
1 teaspoon	powdered ginger
1 tablespoon	soy sauce
12	medium flour tortillas
1 small jar	sweet-and-sour sauce

Preheat oven to 350 degrees.

In a skillet, brown hash browns in butter. Add peas, onion, pineapple, ginger, and soy sauce. Sauté 5 minutes. Place ¼ cup mixture onto each flour tortilla. Fold in the ends of tortilla and roll the sides to form a bundle. Spray 9 x 13-inch pan with nonstick cooking spray. Place each bundle seam-side down. Bake 15 minutes, then turn over. Bake 10 minutes more. Serve hot with sweet-and-sour sauce for dipping.

Slow Cooker Burrito Bake
MAKES 8 SERVINGS

1 pound	lean ground beef
1 envelope	taco seasoning
1	medium onion, chopped
1	green pepper, chopped
1 can (16 ounces)	black beans, with liquid
1 can (16 ounces)	pinto beans, with liquid
2 cans (10 ounces each)	tomatoes and green chiles, drained
10	medium flour tortillas, torn into pieces
4 cups	grated cheddar cheese

Brown ground beef and drain. Stir in taco seasoning. Layer one-third of each ingredient, starting with seasoned beef in the order listed above in a greased 4½- to 6-quart slow cooker. Repeat layers twice more. Cover and cook 6–8 hours on low heat or 3–4 hours on high heat.

Southwest Torta

MAKES 6 SERVINGS

12	corn tortillas
1 teaspoon	garlic powder
1 can (15 ounces)	enchilada sauce
1 can (15 ounces)	black or pinto beans, rinsed and drained
3 cups	grated pepper jack cheese
	sour cream or guacamole

Preheat oven to 400 degrees. Spray a large deep-dish pie pan with nonstick cooking spray. Place 6 tortillas on bottom of pan, overlapping. Add garlic powder to enchilada sauce. Layer half of sauce, beans, and cheese. Then repeat layers, starting with remaining tortillas. Bake for 12–15 minutes. Let stand 5 minutes. Cut into triangle wedges to serve. Garnish with a dollop of sour cream or guacamole.

Sweet-and-Sour Fajitas

MAKES 4 SERVINGS

1 tablespoon	vegetable or olive oil
2	boneless, skinless chicken breasts, cubed
1 bag (16 ounces)	frozen stir-fry vegetables, thawed and drained
$3/4$ cup	sweet-and-sour or stir-fry sauce
8	medium flour tortillas

Heat oil in large frying pan or wok. Add cubed chicken to hot oil, stirring frequently until chicken is thoroughly cooked. Add vegetables to chicken. Stir 2–3 minutes, or until vegetables are cooked through. Drain any excess liquid. Stir in sauce and cook 2 minutes more. Serve in warm flour tortillas.

Tex-Mex Meat Loaf
MAKES 6–8 SERVINGS

2	lightly beaten eggs
8	corn tortillas, pulverized in food processor
½ cup	finely chopped onion
¼ cup	chopped green pepper or green chiles
1 tablespoon	chili powder (optional)
1 teaspoon	salt
2 pounds	lean ground beef
1 cup	ketchup

Preheat oven to 350 degrees. Mix all ingredients together except ketchup. Shape into two small loaves. Place in a 9 x 13-inch pan. Pour ketchup over top. Bake for 60 minutes.

Tortilla Beef Cannelloni

MAKES 4–6 SERVINGS

1 jar (16 ounces)	spaghetti sauce
1 pound	lean ground beef
1 teaspoon	garlic salt
1 tablespoon	Italian seasoning
1 cup	grated mozzarella cheese
12	medium flour tortillas
	Parmesan cheese

Preheat oven to 375 degrees. Spread 3 tablespoons spaghetti sauce in a 9 x 13-inch pan. Brown and drain beef. Add garlic salt, Italian seasoning, and mozzarella cheese. Cut tortillas into 6-inch squares. Place 2 tablespoons beef along one edge of a tortilla square. Roll up, jelly roll style, and place seam-side down in pan. Repeat process with each tortilla square. Pour remaining sauce over top. Bake for 30 minutes. Garnish with Parmesan.

Nacho Sloppy Joes

MAKES 6 SERVINGS

1 pound	**ground turkey or beef**
1 can (6 ounces)	**tomato paste**
1 cup	**water**
1 envelope	**sloppy joe seasoning mix**
1	**small bag tortilla chips**
1 can (6 ounces)	**sliced olives**
2 cups	**grated cheddar cheese**

Brown and drain meat; add tomato paste, water, and seasoning. Simmer 10 minutes, or until thick. Spread tortilla chips on individual plates and spoon sloppy joe mixture over top. Sprinkle with sliced olives and cheese.

Tortilla-Crusted Fish Fillets

MAKES 4 SERVINGS

1	egg mixed with
	1 tablespoon water
1 cup	seasoned bread crumbs
1 cup	finely crushed tortilla chips
4 (4-ounce)	fish fillets
	butter

Preheat oven to 400 degrees. Place egg mixture, crumbs, and tortilla chips on separate plates or bowls. Dip fish fillets, one at a time, in egg mixture, bread crumbs, and crushed tortilla chips in that order. Sauté each fish fillet in buttered frying pan on high heat, 1 minute on each side. Transfer fish fillets to casserole dish. Bake for 20–30 minutes.

Tortilla Spinach and Cheese Cannelloni

MAKES 6 SERVINGS

1 jar (16 ounces)	**Alfredo sauce**
1 package (10 ounces)	**frozen chopped spinach**
1 teaspoon	**garlic salt**
1 tablespoon	**Italian seasoning**
1 cup	**grated mozzarella cheese**
1 cup	**ricotta cheese**
12	**medium flour tortillas**
1	**egg**
	Parmesan cheese, for garnish

Preheat oven to 375 degrees. Spread 3 tablespoons Alfredo sauce in a lightly greased 9 x 13-inch pan.

Sauté spinach in a frying pan. Stir in garlic salt, Italian seasoning, mozzarella and ricotta cheeses, and egg.

Cut tortillas into 6-inch squares. Place 2 tablespoons mixture along one edge of a tortilla square. Roll up and place seam-side down in pan. Repeat for each tortilla square. Pour remaining sauce over tortillas. Bake for 30 minutes. Garnish with Parmesan cheese.

Vegetarian Taco Casserole

MAKES 6 SERVINGS

1 can (15 ounces)	black beans, drained and rinsed
1 can (15 ounces)	ranchero-style pinto beans, with liquid
1 cup	salsa
½ cup	sour cream
2 teaspoons	chili powder
3 cups	crushed tortilla chips
2 cups	grated cheddar cheese
2 cups	shredded lettuce
1	medium tomato, chopped

Preheat oven to 350 degrees. Mix beans, salsa, sour cream, and chili powder. Layer half of bean mixture, chips, and cheese in that order. Repeat layers. Bake 20–30 minutes, or until bubbly. Serve topped with lettuce and tomato.

#74-87

MEXICAN
FAVORITES

Chicken Soft Tacos

MAKES 4–6 SERVINGS

4	boneless, skinless chicken breasts
1 tablespoon	vegetable oil
1	medium onion, chopped
1 jar (16 ounces)	chunky salsa
2 tablespoons	taco seasoning
1½ cups	cheddar or Monterey Jack cheese
10 to 12	small flour tortillas
	sour cream or guacamole

Place chicken in a saucepan and add enough water to cover. Bring to a boil. Simmer over medium-high heat 30 minutes, or until chicken is easy to shred. Reserve ½ cup chicken broth from pan where chicken cooked. Shred chicken using two forks, and set aside.

Heat oil in a frying pan over medium heat. Add onion to oil and cook until translucent. Stir chicken, salsa, taco seasoning, and ½ cup reserved chicken broth into onion. Simmer, uncovered, over low heat 25 minutes, or until thick. Sprinkle cheese over chicken and serve in warm flour tortillas. Garnish with sour cream or guacamole.

If starting recipe with frozen chicken, boil chicken 45 minutes, or until it is ready to shred.

Shredded Beef Tacos
MAKES 8–10 SERVINGS

2 pounds	round steak
2 tablespoons	minced garlic
1 tablespoon	chili powder
1 tablespoon	beef broth granules
12	taco shells
2	tomatoes, chopped
2 cups	grated cheddar cheese
1/2	head iceberg lettuce, finely shredded
	salsa

Remove visible fat from meat. Place in a lightly greased 3½- to 5-quart slow cooker. Add garlic. Cover and cook on low heat 6–8 hours. Shred meat using two forks. Add chili powder and beef broth granules. Leave in slow cooker another 30–60 minutes, stirring as necessary to remove moisture. Set out remaining ingredients in separate bowls and let individuals assemble their own tacos.

Chicken Flautas
MAKES 6–8 SERVINGS

18	corn tortillas
2 cans (10 ounces each)	white chicken meat*
1 teaspoon	cumin
1 cup	grated Monterey Jack cheese
1 can (4 ounces)	diced green chiles
	oil
	guacamole, salsa, or sour cream

Soften tortillas in microwave 60 seconds. Remove and cover with a dish towel to keep tortillas warm and soft. Combine chicken, cumin, cheese, and chiles.

Heat oil 1 inch deep in a small frying pan over medium heat. Place 2 tablespoons chicken mixture in a tortilla, spread vertically about 1 inch from center on one side of tortilla. Roll up jelly roll style. Using tongs, hold seam-side down for about 60 seconds in hot oil. Release and let cook 2–3 minutes more, or until crisp and brown. Roll each tortilla and repeat process. Garnish with guacamole, salsa, or sour cream.

*2 cups diced cooked chicken may be substituted.

Spicy Pork Tacos

MAKES 8–10 SERVINGS

3- to 4-pound	**boneless pork loin roast**
¼ teaspoon	**garlic salt**
1 can (10 ounces)	**hot green enchilada sauce**
10 to 12	**medium flour tortillas**

Place roast in a greased 3½- to 5-quart slow cooker. Sprinkle roast with garlic salt and pour enchilada sauce over top. Cover and cook on low heat 8–10 hours. An hour before serving, shred meat using two forks and continue to cook on low heat, uncovered, for remaining time. Serve in warm flour tortillas with your favorite taco toppings.

Chicken Enchilada Casserole
MAKES 6 SERVINGS

12	corn tortillas
1 can (10.5 ounces)	cream of chicken soup, condensed
1 can (10.5 ounces)	cream of mushroom soup, condensed
1 cup	sour cream or plain yogurt
1 cup	finely chopped green onion
1/2 cup	chopped green chiles
3 cups	grated cheddar cheese, divided
3 cups	cubed cooked chicken

Preheat oven to 325 degrees. Cut or tear tortillas into bite-size pieces. Combine soups, sour cream, onion, chiles, and half of cheese. Spread a little of soup mixture in bottom of a 9 x 13-inch pan. Layer with half of tortillas, chicken, and soup mixture. Repeat layer and top with remaining cheese. Bake for 60 minutes.

#79

Mexican Corn Tortilla Pizzas

MAKES 4–6 SERVINGS

1 tablespoon	vegetable or canola oil
6	corn tortillas
1 pound	ground beef
1	small onion, chopped
1 envelope	taco seasoning
1 can (16 ounces)	refried beans, heated
2 cups	grated cheddar cheese
	diced tomatoes, green chiles, avocado, or sour cream

Preheat oven to 350 degrees. In a large frying pan, heat vegetable oil. Place a tortilla in hot oil. Fry 20 seconds on each side. Remove tortilla from pan and blot with a paper towel to remove excess grease. Repeat for remaining tortillas. Arrange tortillas on two baking sheets.

Wipe excess grease from frying pan and brown beef and onion together until beef is done and onion is translucent. Drain, if necessary. Stir seasoning into meat. Spread a layer of refried beans over entire surface of each tortilla. Evenly divide meat mixture over tortillas. Sprinkle cheese over top. Bake 20 minutes. Garnish individual pizzas with diced tomatoes, green chiles, avocado, or sour cream.

Tortilla Chip Casserole

MAKES 6 SERVINGS

1 pound	ground beef, browned and drained
1 cup	salsa
½ cup	sour cream
2 teaspoons	chili powder
3 cups	crushed tortilla chips
2 cups	grated cheddar cheese
2 cups	shredded lettuce
1	medium tomato, chopped

Preheat oven to 350 degrees. Mix together ground beef, salsa, sour cream, and chili powder. Layer half of meat mixture, chips, and cheese. Repeat layers. Bake 20–30 minutes, or until bubbly. Serve topped with lettuce and tomato.

Classic Enchiladas
MAKES 6 SERVINGS

12	**corn tortillas**
½ cup	**butter**
1 can (30 ounces)	**enchilada sauce**
1 can (4 ounces)	**tomato paste**
4 cups	**grated cheddar cheese**

Preheat oven to 350 degrees. Cook one tortilla at a time in a small frying pan in about 1 teaspoon of butter until tortillas are soft and pliable. Mix enchilada sauce and tomato paste. Spread 1 cup of sauce mixture in bottom of a 9 x 13-inch pan. Roll ⅓ cup cheese in each tortilla jelly roll style and place seam-side down in pan. Pour remaining sauce over top. Bake 30–40 minutes, or until bubbly.

Variation: Use only half the cheese and add meat, such as chicken with green chiles or shredded beef with jalapeños.

Classic Burritos
MAKES 6 SERVINGS

3 cups	diced cooked chicken or beef
6	large flour tortillas
1 can (30 ounces)	refried beans
3 cups	grated cheddar cheese
1 cup	salsa, plus more for garnish
	guacamole
	sour cream

Cook and season meat as desired. Place a tortilla in microwave 20–30 seconds, or until softened. Spread $\frac{1}{2}$ cup beans, $\frac{1}{2}$ cup cheese, $\frac{1}{2}$ cup meat, and a spoonful of salsa in a rectangle along one side of each tortilla. Fold in sides and roll up burrito style. Garnish with guacamole, salsa, and sour cream.

Variation: To make chimichangas, make burritos as directed above. Then heat some canola oil over medium heat in a frying pan. With tongs, place burrito seam-side down in oil and hold 1 minute. Release tongs and cook 1–2 minutes, or until browned. Turn over and cook 1–2 minutes more. Remove from oil and blot with paper towel.

Classic Fajitas
MAKES 6 SERVINGS

¼ cup	lime juice
1 tablespoon	soy sauce
1 tablespoon	olive oil
1 tablespoon	minced garlic
1 teaspoon	white pepper
1 pound	round steak, sliced in ¼-inch strips
1	yellow or purple onion
1 each	red, green, and yellow peppers
½ cup	canola oil
12	medium flour tortillas

Mix lime juice, soy sauce, olive oil, garlic, and white pepper together. Pour mixture over meat and marinate, covered, at least 4 hours or overnight. Cut onion and peppers into ¼-inch strips. Heat oil in large frying pan until very hot. Add meat and stir frequently. When meat loses its pink color, add onion and peppers. Sauté until vegetables are cooked through but not limp. While sizzling, serve with flour tortillas to roll individually.

Variation: Most meats and vegetables are excellent cooked in the same style as directed above. Possible combinations are shrimp or whitefish fillets with mushrooms and onion, chicken strips with zucchini, or veggie fajitas with a variety of vegetables.

Green Chile Burritos

MAKES 6–8 SERVINGS

2 pounds	lean boneless pork roast, cubed
2 tablespoons	minced garlic
1 can (10 ounces)	tomatoes and green chiles, with liquid
1 can (4 ounces)	chopped green chiles
	chili powder and salt, to taste
8	medium flour tortillas
	guacamole, sour cream, and/or salsa

Put pork and garlic in a lightly greased 4½- to 6-quart slow cooker. Cover and cook on low heat 8–10 hours, or on high heat 4–6 hours. Add tomatoes and green chiles and cook 1 hour more on high uncovered. Season with chili powder and salt. Place about ½ cup mixture on each tortilla, roll up, and serve. Garnish with guacamole, sour cream, and/or salsa.

Tortillas in Black Bean Sauce

MAKES 6 SERVINGS

1 can (15 ounces)	black beans, rinsed and drained
1 can (19 ounces)	enchilada sauce
18	corn tortillas
$\frac{1}{2}$ cup	butter
1 container or bag (12 ounces)	queso fresco, crumbled
1 cup	chopped fresh cilantro
2	medium tomatoes, chopped

Blend beans and enchilada sauce in blender until smooth. Sauté each tortilla in a little butter until firm but not crisp. Spread tortillas, one at a time, with black bean sauce on one side. Fold in half and then in half again. Arrange 3 folded tortilla triangles on the center of each serving plate. Spread all 3 tortillas with more sauce. Microwave $1\frac{1}{2}$–3 minutes, or until heated through, and sprinkle with a little queso fresco, cilantro, and tomatoes.

Mom's White Enchiladas

MAKES 6 SERVINGS

¼ cup	flour
½ cup	butter, divided
3 cups	chicken broth
1 can (12 ounces)	diced green chiles
1 container (16 ounces)	sour cream
12	corn tortillas
	butter, for sautéing
1 pound	grated Monterey Jack cheese
6 to 8	green onions, chopped

Preheat oven to 350 degrees. Cook flour in ¼ cup butter in a large frying pan until golden brown; then add broth. Cook over medium heat until thickened, about 5 minutes. Remove from heat and stir in green chiles and sour cream. Spread 1 cup of sauce in bottom of a 9 x 13-inch pan and set the rest aside to cool.

Sauté tortillas in remaining butter until firm but not crisp. Roll up ⅓ cup cheese and 1 tablespoon green onions in a tortilla jelly roll style. Repeat for remaining tortillas, placing each seam-side down in pan. Pour remaining sauce over top. Bake 40–50 minutes, or until bubbly.

Spicy Double-Decker Tacos

MAKES 3–4 SERVINGS

1 pound	ground beef
1 envelope	taco seasoning
1 can (10 ounces)	diced tomatoes and green chilies, with liquid
6 to 8	taco shells
6 to 8	small flour tortillas
1¼ cups	grated cheddar cheese
1½ cups	shredded lettuce
	salsa and sour cream

In a frying pan, brown and drain ground beef. Stir in taco seasoning and tomatoes. Cover and cook over low heat 10 minutes. Place a flour tortilla inside each hard taco shell. Place a scoop of meat mixture into each flour tortilla. Sprinkle a small amount of cheese over meat, then put shredded lettuce over top. Garnish with salsa and sour cream.

DESSERTS

Cherry Enchiladas
MAKES 6 SERVINGS

1 can (21 ounces)	cherry pie filling
6	medium flour tortillas
½ cup	butter or margarine
½ cup	sugar
½ cup	brown sugar
½ cup	water

Spread pie filling evenly down the centers of tortillas. Fold both ends over filling, then roll up jelly roll style to form enchiladas. Place seam-side down in a lightly greased 8 x 8-inch or 9 x 9-inch pan.

In a saucepan, melt butter. Add sugar, brown sugar, and water. Stirring constantly, bring mixture to a boil. Reduce to medium-low heat and simmer 2–3 minutes. Pour sauce over enchiladas.

Preheat oven to 350 degrees. Allow sauce time to return to room temperature before baking enchiladas. Bake 15–20 minutes, or until light golden brown. Serve warm with a scoop of vanilla ice cream.

Variation: Any flavor pie filling may be substituted.

Banana Quesadillas
MAKES 6–8 SERVINGS

1 package (8 ounces)	cream cheese, softened
½ cup	sugar
1 teaspoon	vanilla
4	bananas
8	medium flour tortillas cinnamon sugar, whipped topping, or caramel and chocolate sauce

Mix cream cheese, sugar, and vanilla. Mash 2 bananas and stir into cream cheese mixture. Spread ½ cup banana mixture on half of each tortilla. Place flour tortilla in a nonstick frying pan over medium low heat. Slice remaining bananas and add 5 to 6 slices over top of banana mixture. Fold plain half of tortilla over top, forming a half circle. Cook, turning about every 30 seconds until tortilla is light golden brown on both sides. Serve warm with cinnamon sugar, whipped topping, or caramel and chocolate sauce over top.

Chocolate Raspberry Burritos

MAKES 8 SERVINGS

2 cups	semi-sweet chocolate chips
2 cups	fresh or frozen raspberries
8	medium flour tortillas
4 tablespoons	butter, melted
4 tablespoons	sugar
2 teaspoons	cinnamon

Preheat oven to 425 degrees. Place ¼ cup chocolate chips and ¼ cup raspberries in the center of a tortilla. Fold edges in and roll up to form a burrito. Bake seam-side down on a baking sheet 20 minutes, or until light golden brown. Remove from heat and brush with melted butter; then sprinkle with sugar and cinnamon.

Cinnamon Crisps

MAKES 3–4 SERVINGS

6	**small, medium, or large flour tortillas**
¼ cup	**sugar**
1 teaspoon	**cinnamon**
	fruit salsa or fruit dip

Preheat oven to 400 degrees. Lightly sprinkle tortillas with water. Combine sugar and cinnamon, and sprinkle over tortillas. Cut each tortilla into eight wedges. Place wedges in a single layer on lightly greased baking sheet. Bake 8–10 minutes, or until light golden brown and crisp. Serve with fruit salsa or your favorite fruit dip.

Tortilla Cannolis

MAKES 4–6 SERVINGS

	canola oil, for deep frying
8	medium flour tortillas
⅓ cup	sugar, mixed with 2 teaspoons cinnamon
1 cup	ricotta cheese
1 cup	sugar-free chunky fruit jam or fresh pureed fruit
1 bag (16 ounces)	chocolate chips, melted whipped topping, for garnish

Heat oil in a deep fryer until very hot. Roll up each flour tortilla, leaving a hollow center, and fasten with a toothpick. Deep fry until golden brown. Remove from heat and, using tongs, roll immediately in sugar mixture. Mix ricotta cheese and jam. Fill tortilla shell with cheese mixture. Place on serving plate, drizzle with melted chocolate, and top with a dollop of whipped topping.

Mexican Apple Strudel

MAKES 6–8 SERVINGS

6 cups	peeled and grated cooking apples
1 cup	raisins
1 tablespoon	lemon juice
1 cup	sugar
1 tablespoon	cinnamon
1 cup	chopped nuts
8	medium flour tortillas
½ cup	butter, melted
	whipped topping (optional)

Preheat oven to 350 degrees. Mix apples, raisins, lemon juice, sugar, cinnamon, and nuts. Microwave each tortilla 20 seconds to soften. Spread 1 cup apple mixture on tortilla. Roll up jelly roll style. Wrap tightly with plastic wrap and chill 1 hour. Remove plastic wrap and cut into 1½-inch slices. Place on baking sheet and secure with toothpicks. Brush generously with butter. Bake for 30 minutes. Serve with a dollop of whipped topping, if desired.

Dessert Nachos with Fruit Salsa

MAKES 4–6 SERVINGS

	Cinnamon Crisps (see page 111)
1 package (8 ounces)	cream cheese, softened
¼ cup	orange juice
4 cups	chopped fresh fruit, such as strawberries, kiwi, peaches, mango

Arrange cinnamon crisps on a plate. Mix cream cheese and orange juice together. Drizzle cream cheese mixture over Cinnamon Crisps. Sprinkle fresh chopped fruit over top.

Southwest Bread Pudding
MAKES 8 SERVINGS

3	eggs
3 cups	milk
½ cup	sugar
1 teaspoon	ground nutmeg
1 tablespoon	cinnamon
¼ cup	butter, melted
1 tablespoon	vanilla
¼ cup	raisins
1 cup	chocolate chips
8	slices stale white bread, torn into pieces (about 6 cups)
3	medium flour tortillas, torn into pieces (about 2 cups)
	whipped topping or ice cream (optional)

Preheat oven to 350 degrees. Mix eggs with a fork in a large mixing bowl. Add milk, sugar, spices, butter, and vanilla. Place raisins, chocolate chips, bread, and tortillas in a large mixing bowl and toss; then spread in a 1½-quart baking dish. Pour egg mixture over top. Let stand 30–60 minutes. Bake 30 minutes, or until golden brown on top. Remove from oven and sprinkle with additional sugar and cinnamon. Serve warm with a dollop of whipped topping or ice cream, if desired.

Lattice-Top Peach Cobbler

MAKES 6–8 SERVINGS

¼ cup	butter
½ cup	sugar
2 tablespoons	flour
1 tablespoon	cinnamon
8 cups	sliced peaches*
4	large flour tortillas

Preheat oven to 350 degrees. Melt butter in a 2-quart casserole dish. Mix together sugar, flour, and cinnamon, and toss with peaches. Spread peaches on top of butter. Wet tortillas under running water. Place 2 tortillas together and cut into 1-inch strips. Weave over top of peaches, lattice-style. Repeat with remaining tortillas. Entire dish should be covered with tortilla strips. Bake for 30–40 minutes.

*Drained canned peaches may be used in this recipe.

Hot Fudge Tostada

MAKES 4 SERVINGS

4	medium gordita-style flour tortillas
	cinnamon and sugar
6 cups	vanilla ice cream, divided
1 jar	hot fudge ice cream topping

Center tortilla in a microwave-safe cereal bowl. Press tortilla down to form the shape of the bowl. Microwave 30 seconds. Remove and press down air pockets that have formed. Microwave an additional 30 seconds. Remove tortilla and place on a tray where it can continue to dry out. Repeat process for remaining tortillas. Sprinkle cinnamon and sugar inside bottom of tortilla bowl. Place 2 or 3 scoops of ice cream in tortilla bowl. Heat hot fudge according to directions and drizzle over ice cream.

Strawberry Margarita Squares
MAKES 10–12 SERVINGS

Crust:

1½ cups	finely crushed tortilla chips
¼ cup	melted butter
1 tablespoon	sugar

Filling:

1 can (14 ounces)	sweetened condensed milk
2 cups	pureed strawberries
½ cup	lime juice
1 container (8 ounces)	frozen whipped topping, thawed
	sliced strawberries, for garnish

Mix crust ingredients together and press into a 9 x 13-inch pan. Mix together sweetened condensed milk, pureed strawberries, and lime juice. Gently fold whipped topping into strawberry mixture and pour over top of crust. Freeze 4–6 hours. Let stand at room temperature 15 minutes before serving. Cut into squares and garnish with fresh sliced strawberries.

Strawberry Shortilla

MAKES 6 SERVINGS

1½ cups	sugar, divided
8 cups	sliced strawberries
12	medium flour tortillas
¼ cup	butter
½ cup	sugar
1 container (8 ounces)	whipped topping, thawed

Add 1 cup sugar to sliced strawberries and let sit 20–30 minutes. Cut tortillas into 3- to 4-inch circles, using a small bowl as a guide. Sauté each tortilla circle in 1 teaspoon butter until lightly crisp. Using tongs, remove from frying pan and sprinkle each side with 1 teaspoon sugar. Place 1 tortilla circle on a plate. Top with ½ cup strawberries. Place another tortilla circle on top and top with ½ cup more strawberries. Top with a large dollop of whipped topping.

Upside-Down Apple Pie
MAKES 6–8 SERVINGS

½ cup	butter, divided
½ cup	brown sugar, divided
1 cup	chopped pecans
2	large flour tortillas
½ cup	sugar
¼ cup	flour
1 teaspoon	cinnamon
6 cups	sliced peeled tart apples*
	ice cream (optional)

Preheat oven to 350 degrees. Spray an 8-inch pie pan with nonstick cooking spray. Line pie pan with wax paper. Mix ¼ cup butter, ¼ cup brown sugar, and pecans; spread over wax paper in bottom of pie pan. Place 1 tortilla over top. Combine rest of ingredients except remaining tortilla and ice cream. Spread evenly in pie pan. Place tortilla over top. Press down to remove air pockets. Cut slits in tortilla. Bake 60–80 minutes, or until golden brown and heated through. Remove and cool 20–30 minutes. Invert onto a serving plate and remove wax paper. Serve immediately with ice cream, if desired.

*Approximately 6 large apples.

S'mores Nachos

MAKES 4 SERVINGS

	Cinnamon Crisps (see page 111)
½ cup	**caramel sauce**
20 to 30	**mini marshmallows**
2	**chocolate candy bars, broken into pieces**
1 cup	**graham cracker crumbs**

Spread Cinnamon Crisps on a 9 x 13-inch pan or oven-proof platter. Drizzle caramel sauce and sprinkle marshmallows and chocolate pieces over top. Place on center rack of oven and broil 3–5 minutes, or until light golden brown and bubbly. Remove from oven and sprinkle with graham cracker crumbs.

NOTES

NOTES

NOTES

NOTES

NOTES

Metric Conversion Chart

VOLUME MEASUREMENTS		WEIGHT MEASUREMENTS		TEMPERATURE CONVERSION	
U.S.	Metric	U.S.	Metric	Fahrenheit	Celsius
1 teaspoon	5 ml	½ ounce	15 g	250	120
1 tablespoon	15 ml	1 ounce	30 g	300	150
¼ cup	60 ml	3 ounces	90 g	325	160
⅓ cup	75 ml	4 ounces	115 g	350	180
½ cup	125 ml	8 ounces	225 g	375	190
⅔ cup	150 ml	12 ounces	350 g	400	200
¾ cup	175 ml	1 pound	450 g	425	220
1 cup	250 ml	2¼ pounds	1 kg	450	230

About the Authors

Stephanie Ashcraft was raised in Indiana. She received a bachelor's degree in family science and a teaching certificate from Brigham Young University. Stephanie loves teaching, interacting with people, and spending time with friends and family. She has taught hundreds of classes and appeared on hundreds of television and news programs all over the country sharing ways families can save time and money in the kitchen. Stephanie and her husband, Ivan, reside in Salem, Utah, with their five children.

Donna Kelly, a food fanatic and recipe developer, is the author of many cookbooks including *Quesadillas*, *French Toast*, *Burritos*, *101 Things to Do with Tofu*, and *101 Things to Do with an Air Fryer*. She lives in Salt Lake City, Utah.